T0193338

THE
LOVE
REVOLUTION

A Meditation Journey to Love

ERIN LEWIS

BALBOA.
PRESS
A DIVISION OF HAY HOUSE

This book is a work of non-fiction. Unless otherwise noted, the author and the publisher make no explicit guarantees as to the accuracy of the information contained in this book and in some cases, names of people and places have been altered to protect their privacy.

Balboa Press books may be ordered through booksellers or by contacting:

Balboa Press
A Division of Hay House
1663 Liberty Drive
Bloomington, IN 47403
www.balboapress.com
1 (877) 407-4847

Because of the dynamic nature of the Internet, any web addresses or links contained in this book may have changed since publication and may no longer be valid. The views expressed in this work are solely those of the author and do not necessarily reflect the views of the publisher, and the publisher hereby disclaims any responsibility for them.

The author of this book does not dispense medical advice or prescribe the use of any technique as a form of treatment for physical, emotional, or medical problems without the advice of a physician, either directly or indirectly. The intent of the author is only to offer information of a general nature to help you in your quest for emotional and spiritual well-being. In the event you use any of the information in this book for yourself, which is your constitutional right, the author and the publisher assume no responsibility for your actions.

Any people depicted in stock imagery provided by Getty Images are models, and such images are being used for illustrative purposes only. Certain stock imagery © Getty Images.

Print information available on the last page.

ISBN: 978-1-9822-0267-5 (sc)
ISBN: 978-1-9822-0269-9 (hc)
ISBN: 978-1-9822-0268-2 (e)

Library of Congress Control Number: 2018904950

Balboa Press rev. date: 05/09/2018

CONTENTS

This book is dedicated to my daughters, I would not be me without you three! Stay grounded and fly high my lovelies.

INTRODUCTION

I AM ERIN JOY Lewis, and Joy is in my name. I wasn't born with it; I chose it as a nod to my lifelong mission to seek out and ground the energy of love. My meditation journey began 30 years ago. I live in a beautiful place that allows me splendid isolation. It's perfect for a meditating missionary.

I am a Yoga Teacher and a Family Constellation Facilitator. I help people remove blocks and clear resistance that stands between them and love, for themselves and their families. I have spent my life studying and teaching ways that help love flow in bodies, minds, and souls; enabling seekers to gain freedom from limitation and find new possibilities. My purpose is always to find ways to allow love to shine through.

For thousands of years, meditation has been used as a vehicle to reach spiritual heights. I have practiced many different styles of meditation throughout my lifelong spiritual journey and the decades of study. I have stared at candles, and I have listened to chants. I have prayed, and I have repeated mantras. I have battled with thought and I have directed thought. I have sat with Tibetan monks in the Himalayas. I have visited the stars and traveled to the center of the earth. I have practiced moving meditation and singing meditation. I have used crystals, Tibetan bowls, affirmations and creative visualization. I have tried it all.

Over the last few years, I surrendered all of these practices. I stopped seeking an outside source of love and allowed myself to come home to *love in my self.* Loving myself.

Over the years I have discovered a system, or should I say a system discovered me, and here it is. "The Love Revolution."

What follows in this book is a framework, a container to hold the body, the mind and the heart in a grounded, loving way. It has been my divine pleasure to write this little book.

A source of Source.

All You Need Is Love

WELCOME ABOARD

A NEW CONSCIOUSNESS IS arising on our planet and with it a movement towards love. We live in exciting times! There is scientific proof that our hearts are stronger than our brains and that our emotionally charged thoughts create our lives. To access this power, we have to find a way to step out of the physical, emotional, and mental stress of life and connect to love. We can do this by becoming conscious of our blocks to love, and with meditation. This book will show you how, and by guiding you step-by-step, you will become a beacon of love.

To begin your Love Revolution, I am asking you to commit to being kind to yourself and to love yourself - no matter what. Only then can you unchain your heart and walk in love. The Love Revolution is a sacred journey, as we walk in the light of divine Source/God force energy. This process, therefore, meant to be taken lightly.

At times, it won't be easy, but it won't be boring. It will be an intrepid journey that has the potential to be life-changing. Every day will be different. Some days on your travels, you may find heaven on earth, and some days you will feel like you are in hell. Some days will be full of busyness, and some days will be divinely blank. Some days will be uncomfortable, and some days will be bliss. Some days you will lose time and sit in meditation longer than you thought possible. And some days you will wiggle and jiggle for what feels like an eternity but find it was only ten minutes. It is all part of the journey.

You will need to be openhearted as you review, and reset your habitual thought patterns. There will be days when you find yourself sitting in the shadows, as love brings up to the light everything that is unlike itself. Your hidden stuff will surface. Fantastic! Be aware that this may throw you off balance and you may trip. It is all part of the journey. Take a deep breath, and forgive yourself for the fall.

Treat yourself kindly when the journey appears difficult, even though your natural instinct will be to give yourself a hard time. These tricky times are when you must give yourself *more* love, not less. Trust yourself, and have faith that you can do it. I know you can do it. I believe in your full potential, and it is this part of you that I write.

Feel free to take some, if not all, of the words in these pages for yourself. Some of the words will resonate immediately, and some may take a little longer. If you are curious, read the book through and then go back to the beginning to start the Love Revolution meditation. I recommend you take one chapter on board a week, and then practice, practice, practice. The first week isn't a sit-down meditation; it's two exercises to ready you for the weeks ahead. A simple statement and a breathing exercise. Do not race through the steps. A strong foundation leads to a strong structure, and a strong structure leads to a strong revolution.

Use this book as a study guide, take a highlighter (or a pen) to these pages, and make these words, and this book your own. Be creative. Add notes and circle pieces that ring true. Own it!

You may want to encourage friends to get a copy of this book for themselves so they can go on this journey with you. Or you could organize a group to meditate, discuss, and support each other. It is a fabulous idea to share your journey as it helps ground it. You could even start your own neighborhood Love Revolution!

However you choose to make this journey, alone or with travel buddies, the first step is always the hardest. You have to make some decisions. You have to decide to gift yourself a few minutes every day, over the next month, to the Love Revolution. You have to decide to open yourself to love, and you have to decide to receive it. You have to decide that there is no one on the planet more deserving of your love than *you*.

"I LOVE MYSELF!"

Generally, we are hard on ourselves. We hold high expectations, or none at all, and judge ourselves harshly. We are our own worst critics. We criticize ourselves in the mirror, and we doubt our ability to succeed.

To tune yourself into love, I want you to take on board a short statement to say silently, and out loud whenever you can. I am asking you to repeat it frequently until it becomes automatic. At first, it may seem difficult, and in fact darn right silly, to be saying this to yourself. If you stick with it for the month it will take to read and practice the Love Revolution; you *will* be forever changed. I promise!

The magic words are "I love myself!"

Make this the mantra that you repeat regularly, out loud and internally, until it becomes a new belief. Your subconscious mind listens to and believes wholeheartedly everything you think and say, so be aware of what you are saying about yourself because *you* are always listening.

When you state, "I love myself!" new neural pathways will be created in your brain so that you *will* love yourself. Once you believe it, every cell in your body will hear it, and they will believe it too. You will glow with love and be lovely to behold. Your love will radiate out into the world, and you will see proof of your belief as the world shows you how it loves you back. Your life will become a manifestation of love.

Be warned that you will find inevitable resistance to your new notion. You have spent years telling yourself how unlovable you are. You may not know what it means to be loved. You may not believe you deserve love.

Keep practicing; say it anyway. It may feel odd in the beginning, but you will get used to it. If you find your mind arguing with you, to prove how unlovable you are, spend the first week repeating "I love myself for practicing to love myself!" Don't you love that?

Loving yourself is a total win/win. By loving yourself, you will feel self-confidence and inner peace, meaning you are not relying on others to support you emotionally. You will become self-sufficient and overflow in love, which will feed the field of consciousness around you. It is so incredibly empowering to be full to overflowing with love. It's the highest vibration in existence. It is enlightened.

To be enlightened means to find the light within. Self-love is the true definition of enlightenment. To love you, with all of your flaws, and without judgment or expectation is the key. To accept and appreciate the dramas and traumas you have lived as being necessary steps on your path to being your true self.

I imagine we are all like pearls that grow more beautiful every year by rolling around in the daily grit, within our oyster shells. Right now, the world is your oyster and you, my friend, are the pearl.

Self-love enables you to make healthier choices for your body, mind, and soul. When you love yourself and make decisions from that vibration, you are inviting amazing experiences into your life; you begin to greet your full potential. You are on a path of fulfillment and will be an inspiration to many who will see you glow with new confidence and self-awareness. You will overflow with love and be a pure expression of divine Source/ God force energy.

Love is creative, healthy, and abundant. It is expansive and expressive energy. Tune yourself in like a radio to love. Start by doing loving things for yourself, and then go out and do loving things for others. Be the light in your world. Watch as your stress levels decrease. Then you will begin to release layers of mental and emotional trash, which is energetic clutter. Buried under all that clutter is only love.

Some people around you will think you are a little crazy to be declaring your love for self. Self-love has always been considered selfish and egotistical. We are taught to care for others before ourselves and to be humble. All this does is martyr us and limit our possibilities.

What if we become self-full, not selfish, and encourage others to be self-full too? From this space of power, we are aligned with the universe and living an inspired life. We stop seeking love in all the wrong places and begin to embody love. We become love.

True self-love is not arrogance or putting yourself first. It is not about always looking after number one and having things go your way. It is not a comparison to others, and wondering if you are better than them, or if they are better than you. It is not criticizing those around you, or yourself.

Self-love is about being brave enough to clean out the stuff hidden in the dark, and to love yourself while you do. To self-soothe your Shadow Self with self-love, which allows you to be more available to love others around you. You will be of higher service to all.

The more you love yourself, the more beneficial you are to humanity. Loving ourselves is being on the Love Revolution and marching toward healthy, happy, and whole. Stop and imagine a world full of radiant love revolutionaries humbly practicing meditation and consciously setting their vibration. They fill themselves up with love and radiate love to their families, their communities, their countries, and the planet.

If you decide - and the decision is yours - to find balance and order within your body and your life, you will find it by being part of the Love Revolution. *Decide* is the power word. A decision carries your intention outward to the universe and inward to your soul.

The first step is to look at your stress responses, so you can control and learn to over-ride them.

FIGHT & FLIGHT

We carry fear in our DNA, every animal does. In the good old/bad old days, we had precarious lives and had to protect and defend ourselves constantly. We are still the same physical beings our ancient ancestors were, even though the world we live in has changed dramatically.

Our ancestors had the stress response, fight/flight, as a lifesaving switch. This switch turns off unnecessary systems in an emergency, like the immune and digestive, and directs the energy instead to the heart, lungs, limbs, and our senses. This switch floods us with chemicals to make us stronger and faster. We become hyper-alert and poised for action, to either fight or run. We are wired for survival 24 hours a day, 7 days a week.

We no longer need to have this response to save ourselves from being eaten. But we do still have the lifesaving switch. We have fight/flight response constantly within our modern lives as we rush around feeling stressed by our lists of things to do. Rush, rush, rush! And all that rushing tells our brain that we are running from danger, and so we start pumping stress chemicals.

Stress can either be acute (short-term) or chronic (long-term). We are physically built to handle acute stress, fight/flight and then back to normal restore mode. Chronic stress is when short-term stress has become long-term, and our bodies no longer know how to turn fight/flight off. This chronic stress leads to inflammation in the body, the mind, and in the emotions.

Inflammation is a response to our environment. We commonly think of it as an allergic or toxic response. When we say we are allergic to something, we mean it is poisonous for us. Stress is an allergic reaction to life, and when we have that reaction chronically, stress becomes our everyday reality. We live life in inflammation.

Immune cells get changed under chronic stress and become ready to take on any infection or repair any damage. Unfortunately, they are fired up and ready even when there is nothing to fight. These cells cause inflammation in the body and inflammation causes disease.

Chronic stress in the mind leads to anxiety and insomnia. Stressful thoughts keep looping round and round, tying us up in mental knots. Chronic stress of the emotions gives us an inflamed ego stuck in fear, which makes us anxious and irritable, depressed and with very short fuses, making us overly reactive.

Stress in our modern lives is a perception. It is how we think about our lives that cause stress reactions within our body. We give ourselves stress, nothing else does, even though it is difficult for us to remain detached from outside influences. Look around. People are overreacting to their daily lives; they are attempting to outrun their imagined predators. No one can switch the stress off.

The fight/flight response is an electrical impulse, which is released to charge us up. If we don't express this with fight or flight, this electrical charge causes havoc to our body as stress. Recently there has been acknowledged a third response called 'freeze,' which is the paralyzing terror felt when we realize we can't outfight or outrun our predator. Within that moment the body freezes and is unable to express the emotional and physical release of the fight/flight process.

When we find ourselves in this situation, our body is pumping the chemicals, but we are internalizing all of the responses, like a deer in the headlights. The frozen emotion gets stuck in our mind and our body. Instead of us feeling the emotion and moving through and out of it, it gets stored it in our cells. Emotions are not supposed to be internalized. They are supposed to be experienced, accepted, and then released.

These unexpressed moments can replay throughout our life. All it takes is for some situation to remind us somehow of a trauma we have suffered in our past, and we are triggered. The original fear of that memory resurfaces and plays out in the 'here and now.'

Experts are just beginning to understand the effects of trauma on our systems and our lives, and therefore our families and communities. This understanding becomes more profound when you realize that trauma a grandparent suffered affects their parenting and therefore their children, which goes on to affect the children's parenting and therefore their children, and so on. This pattern is called intergenerational trauma, and all families experience it.

Our parents did the best they could do, with whatever fears, dramas, and traumas they had running. Just like them, we do the best we can.

Trauma can be felt at the loss of a loved one, betrayal, accidents, abuse, violence or being bullied, for example. Some indicating behaviors of fight/flight/freeze response playing out in your life could be as follows.

Fight = anger, rage, nausea, a tight jaw, grinding teeth and a need to argue. Flight = anxiety, excessive energy, restlessness, and tension in the body. Freeze = dread, breath holding, numbness to life, feeling trapped.

No wonder we are all feeling stressed. And this is ordinary! On the Love Revolution, we are leaving ordinary behind, and moving towards extraordinary. You are going to embrace the fear and love yourself anyway. Let's march forward and start to look at emotions.

EMOTIONS

Emotions are energy in motion. E-motion. They are waves of energy moving through us, causing physical and mental responses. And our feelings are expressions of those waves of emotional energy. Because emotions are biochemistry, they can be overridden and reprogrammed. Inflamed emotions do not need to lead to a breakdown; we can use them for a conscious breakthrough. When you are aware that an emotion isn't working for you, there is an opportunity to choose a new emotion, like love, and change your chemistry.

Negative emotions are an invitation to grow up, to grow out and expand. You want to embrace all chances to transmute what presents itself. You are detoxing your emotions. Better out than in! Feel grateful that you have an opportunity to clean up your vibration. And as soon as possible, take yourself away, even if it is by stomping, and find somewhere to sit quietly. Place your hand on your heart, and say, "It is OK. I love you."

You can fake an emotional state to switch your physical state. You can 'fake it until you make it.' Emotions create change within your body faster than anything else. By allowing your brain time to rewire means you will have a period where you know one thing, but you are still reacting to another. It can be tricky at times. When you are triggered, you may not be able to stop your emotional reaction. Things may be negative… that is OK. You are practicing. It's all good! It's all *very* good!

I am not asking you to ignore negative emotions. I am asking you to feel into them and to love yourself anyway. When you are feeling negative, it is easy to give yourself a hard time, but this is when you need some loving. Love is the only way. State to yourself and the Universe, "I love myself even though I feel…"

Loving yourself is having the courage to feel your emotions without judging or criticizing them. It's holding space for yourself when you are feeling sad, angry or lonely with the utmost love and respect. So, greet and welcome your negative emotions, your anger, your grief, and your shame. Own them, so they don't own you.

We are all one in the Universe. We are all connected. We are all a part of the cosmic ocean that energetically surrounds us. The Universe is within us, and we are within the Universe. This simple truth means that we cannot possibly experience pure love without first loving ourselves. So start asking, "Who am I in this moment? Fearful or love full?" Learn your vibrational frequency and become responsible for the energy you bring with you into every situation.

What you believe about yourself is what gets reflected back to you by the world around you. If you are having a lot of negativity thrown at you, you need to have a look at what it is that you are putting out. When you believe you are unworthy, not good enough, people will meet you at that and will take advantage of you. This usually won't be a conscious decision on their part, but just a meeting of vibrations and learned behaviors.

Knowing you are good enough, and even more than good enough radiates as contentment and satisfaction within your life. It gives you self-confidence that is attractive, and you start attracting more circumstances to be content and satisfied with. When you know you are more than enough, and you are full of the love of self, you do not need to judge another, or have any expectations of them. All that fades away, and you let others be whom they need or want to be. Beautiful presence/presents to gift to humanity.

What is it that you express to the world? What are the values you live by? What do you wish to contribute to humankind? These are big questions, and worth answering. Spend some time reflecting on them. Discover what sparks you up. Question yourself. Ask, "What **quest** am **I on**?"

It doesn't matter to me, or the Universe, whether you join the Love Revolution for personal health and healing, or for global peace. As long as you are aligning with love, your input is as equally valuable as another's. No one love is better than another. Love is love.

Be careful to never doubt yourself, you are powerful beyond your comprehension, and stronger than you believe. Doubt is the quickest way to disempower you, never let yourself do it. If you feel doubt arising, stop and take a deep breath, center yourself and tell yourself it is OK. In fact, it is more than OK. Because right here and now, within *this* moment, you are loving yourself. Well done!

Try to do a 'negativity fast,' and encourage those you live with to try it too. Decide only to think and speak positively. It may mean you don't have anything to say when you meet up with family or friends, *but,* saying nothing is better than tuning yourself down with negativity.

Complaining about everything is a habit a lot of people have, it is negative energy aimed at your life. Criticism about others is negativity aimed at someone else. Self-criticism is negativity aimed at you. All of these behaviors are reinforcing negativity. You are giving your power away.

Be aware of your conversations and of the energy of the words you are speaking, and start noticing the conversations in which you are engaged. Fear and worry control a lot of people's lives, and by talking with them at that level, you are allowing that energy to control your life too. Endeavor to change the way you interact in conversation, and acknowledge that you are encountering people, places, and things that are inviting you to look at your negativity. Looking at yourself is how you can change your life, by consciously moving from victim to survivor, to thriver.

SWITCH BREATH

Breath is the elixir of life. If we didn't breathe, we wouldn't live. It's that simple. We are declared dead once we stop breathing. But most of us are shallow breathers and therefore only half full of life force. We breathe lightly or even hold our breath when we are busy, anxious or stressed, depriving our systems of oxygen, which causes inflammation in the body. This shallow chest breathing triggers our stress response, and the release of stress chemicals, which causes us to feel anxious and triggers shallow chest breathing. It is a loop in which we can get caught.

Belly breath switches us to relaxation and restores our chemical balance. Being aware of when we feel stressed is empowering. It is the key to switching from stressed to blessed. Without this awareness, our stress responses run us, and we lose control of our emotions, our thoughts, and our bodies. Breathing deeply into our belly, connects us to ourselves instantly. We stand taller and more relaxed when we breathe deeply. We expand and open.

Check your breath now. Is it stressed or relaxed, fast or slow, shallow or deep, irregular or regular, forced or smooth? By feeling into the body, you are becoming present to yourself and to what you are vibrating out to others. Are you stressed or relaxed? Are you vibrating fear or love? Breath is the indicator of how energetic we are at each given moment. Stressed breathing restricts our energy flow, and relaxed breathing increases it.

Now take some breaths into your belly. When you 'belly breathe' your focus shifts from your mental space into your body space, as you sink out of the external and relax into the internal you. Deep abdominal breathing is the first step in self-healing, the first step in self-connection.

When your awareness is in your belly, you can access your emotions, through your physical body as gut reactions and gut instincts. It is so important to utilize this inner wisdom as the mind may be telling us one thing, but the belly may be telling us something else, and that can only cause our feelings of separation, which is stressful.

Become aware of your body during your day and notice when something makes your body tense. This is a powerful moment, a chance to step out of a contracted closed state and into an open receiving state. We have to be open to receive opportunities.

When we are 'contracted' into a 'safe' space, we will never realize our dreams and our potential. It takes bravery to step out of our comfort zone and into the unknown, but that is where our future expansion lies.

There is a lot of information in these pages, designed to bring up and release fear in the face of love. So, as previously indicated, I would encourage you to practice a chapter per week, adding on to and lengthening your meditation as you go through the book. There is always a space at the end of each session for you to surrender to the experience before you continue. Space to just rest and *be*.

First I want to introduce you to the Switch Breath, which is my favorite trick. It is a short and powerful practice for whenever you find yourself feeling negative or stressed. By practicing the Switch Breath, you will slow your breath, relax your body, calm your mind, and open your heart. This breath throws a switch in the brain, to change from pumping toxic chemicals to tonic chemicals. It is like putting yourself in a love bubble, no matter what is going on around you.

This breathing routine became one of my favorite techniques as I learned and studied Yoga. I gave it the name Switch Breath, and I use this with my therapy clients as well as during Yoga classes. It is an empowering little practice, which takes all of 64 seconds, just over a minute of your time. It can be practiced anywhere by anyone and can be done in public, quickly and quietly.

Play with it and practice the Switch Breath often during your day. No one will know what you are up to, and if they are watching, they will see someone who looks like they are daydreaming. You aren't; you are inwardly focused. Practice it until it is an automatic response to negative energy. Practice it so you can switch your body instantly from stress to bless. Practice it to relax and surrender for a moment.

This week's practice is the "I love myself!" affirmation, and the Switch Breath.

If you get nothing else from this book, get this…

PRACTICE

Find a comfortable seat, on a cushion on the floor, or in a comfortable chair, or even sitting up in bed. Keep your eyes open and softly focus on nothing in particular, like the floor, your hands in your lap or the horizon. Settle into that daydreaming feeling. Become aware of the space you are in by using your peripheral vision, and then become aware of the space you fill, in the space, you are in.

Now focus on your breath. I want you to inhale through the nose to a count of four, hold the full lung for a count of four, exhale through the mouth for a count of four, and hold empty lungs for a count of four. Repeat four times.

Count slowly and steadily, but please do not force the breath or the hold. Find a rhythm that is right for you. As you practice this, your counts will get slower. You are switching off the stress chemicals pumping from the brain, and switching on restorative chemicals. Stressed to blessed!

In for four.
Hold for four.
Out for four.
Hold for four.
Repeat for four.

Allow your breath to settle back to where it feels natural. Use your peripheral vision to acknowledge the space around you, and to acknowledge your place in the space. Feel the restorative, tonic chemicals flooding through your body, bringing relaxation. Feel the relaxation. Notice your body responding to the relaxation chemicals that are starting to flow with this breathing exercise.

The Switch Breath acts like a circuit breaker for the looping, busy energy of the mind and allows you to settle deeply physically. It is also your first meditation practice. Practice this seated, practice this standing, and practice this when you go to bed. Practice this throughout your day, so it becomes second nature. Make the Switch Breath a habit.

This habit will serve you well on the Love Revolution.

When you are ready, move onto the next chapter.

2

GROUND YOURSELF IN LOVE

BODY SPACE

OUR BODY IS THE physical expression of our DNA, who we are and from where we originate. It is what we present to the world, whether we like it or not. It is what our soul inhabits in this lifetime. We are usually unattached to our body and forever in our heads. We take for granted the miraculous creation that we are.

We are an amazing system of trillions of cells, which is continuously realigning and replacing millions of cells every minute. Change is happening within us with every breath. Each of our cells contains a complete blueprint of our DNA.

Every single cell! Take a deep breath here and let that sink in. Again, every single one of our trillions of cells owns a complete blueprint of our unique DNA.

The possibilities within this realization are limitless as we can control our cells with our emotional biochemistry, and therefore influence our DNA. The mind is the cause, and body is the effect of all the thoughts and beliefs we have. Our thoughts create emotions, which create the release of chemicals, and the brain efficiently pumps these chemicals to all of our cells.

When we are stressed, the fight/flight response produces stress hormones into our bloodstream to help us fight and run. But in our daily life, these hormones can run wild, as we are not discharging them like we were made to. Two primary stress hormones affect us. Adrenaline increases our heart rate and elevates our blood pressure, which gives us a hit of energy that we don't usually use. And Cortisol, which increases our blood sugars and fires up our brain, so we can react with speed. Again, we don't often use it.

So we have a power surge rush through our body, which gives us a high, and after the high, there is a low. All those chemicals have to go somewhere, and they do, into our cells. These chemicals keep the cells peaking and crashing with energy. When this process is repeated for a sustained amount of time, we can develop some severe stress disorders.

Too much stress shrinks the part of the brain which stores memories, meaning it is hard to remember things, and also hard to learn. It also makes it extremely difficult to think straight, which is when we instinctively crave sugar and fat, as these are high-energy fuel. But of course, if we are not outrunning a predator, we will just gain weight.

Our immune system gets turned off with the fight/flight response, as does our digestive system, leaving us susceptible to bugs and viruses, and stomach disorders. Add to this the chronic pain from muscles that are tensed for action, and it is enough to stress you out!

Stress creates fear, which creates stress, which creates even more fear, and so it goes...

We have fear as instinctual self-defense, which is good, but not usually necessary. Remember feelings are just energy, and it is OK to express and process these emotions. In fact, it is more than OK! It's a blessing. If we can feel it, we can heal it. We are emptying out and creating new space inside for love.

If it needs to be expressed, then express; if it needs to be processed, then process. But don't wallow. If something is brewing, take the opportunity to release it. Go somewhere quiet and tell yourself you are safe. Punch a pillow or kick on your bed. Dig over your garden. Beat a rug. Go on a nature walk where you can have a yell and a scream. Do what has to be done to allow that energy to move from suppressed to expressed. If you need support, please go and find it from a friend or a therapist.

Transmute that stuff, and love yourself as you do. This process is alchemy in action, turning lead into gold. And it can be fun! In fact, I suggest making noise and stamping often, to allow your body to release.

Stress is a physical and emotional response to fear. Let's call it! Stress is a fearful reaction to life. So next time you feel stressed, ask yourself what you are afraid of. The energy of fear is destructive, to your cells and your confidence, preventing you from reaching your true magnificence, your full potential. The body will produce either stress hormones or restorative hormones; you cannot produce both at the same time. So, if you are always stressed, you are never restoring. Sad but true.

Do not fear the fear. You are safe. And once you know you are safe while working with these emotions, you can work with them in a meditative space by allowing them to flow out of the body, lovingly. It is powerfully transformational, and you will feel old 'stuff' releasing from within your mind and your cells. You will create a new set point for your cells, and therefore your health and your life. You will be happy in your skin, completely independent of outside influences. And that happiness will shine out of you. You will radiate with love. You will have your glow on, and your life will glow too.

DOSE OF PLEASURE

Deep within our brain, we have a pleasure center, which is triggered when we find pleasure by eating delicious food, laughing, having fun, sex and being in love. When we access this center, we release pleasure hormones, which are tonic chemicals for our bodies. We have pleasure wired into the hard-drive of our brain. We are made to be happy and to experience pleasure. If we don't have pleasure in our lives, we feel miserable, tired and unmotivated.

We want the pleasure, but the behaviors that we use to achieve it can be destructive. The chemicals released when we find pleasure are so blissful that we can quickly get addicted to what brings us pleasure. Sex, drugs, and rock and roll. Also, food, shopping, sex, gambling, sugar, and alcohol, to name a few...

Emotions can be addictive too as they release chemicals into our body. Anger, resentment, the 'poor me' story, depression, and other negative feelings, are emotional habits which keep us safe from our pain.

All addictions are being used for pain relief, soothing us by suppressing our feelings. But we have to feel to heal. The

Buddhist scriptures talk about an inner being, which holds our pain, and they call it the hungry ghost. The hungry ghost has a small head with a tiny mouth and an enormous belly. This makes it impossible to fill and leaves it forever hungry. By acknowledging the hungry ghost within us, we can then decide to feel what it is that makes us so emotionally hungry.

Contemplate for a moment, and recognize how you find pleasure. What is it specifically that you do to access pleasure. And then ask yourself whether you are addicted to the things you do to bring pleasure.

There are four primary chemicals that we release with pleasure. **D**opamine, **O**xytocin, **S**erotonin, and **E**ndorphins. When we get a regular DOSE, we improve our mood, renew our cells, boost our immunity and increase our blood circulation. It is like rebooting your system. Pleasure is essential for proper physical and emotional health. It is imperative for a long and happy life to get a daily DOSE, and here are a few simple ways.

Dopamine is released when we are in the sun, doing exercise, or meditating. It is the brain chemical that motivates us and keeps us focused. Oxytocin is released when we experience loving touch, so find a friend or a pet to hug regularly. It is the chemical that gives us the warm fuzzies and reduces anxiety. Serotonin can be released by feeling gratitude for your life and your achievements. It is the chemical that regulates your positive moods and helps you sleep. Endorphins are released with when we laugh out loud, exercise and meditate, and they help us deal with pain and stress. Heard of the runner's high? Well, you are going to learn how to achieve the meditator's high!

Meditation accesses the pleasure center and releases tonic chemicals without external stimulation; meaning instead of searching for pleasure outside of ourselves, we can find it within. The practice of meditation will train your brain to feel happy and naturally high, and even better is that this high does not have a crash following it and becomes the new set point for your brain. Eventually, it can override other high seeking behaviors, allowing you to lose your addictive, pleasure-seeking behaviors by merely meditating and maintaining your daily DOSE. You will also be less perceptible to stress.

Access to the pleasure center through meditation makes it easy to practice daily. You will start to realize the physical, mental and emotional benefits and become 'addicted' to feeling great, which makes you eager to sit in the *now*, making it easy to maintain a daily practice.

It all sounds marvelous, and it is, but how does it relate to your busy mind and life? The thing to realize is 'where' you are in your life right now, never truly defines 'who' you are. You are infinitely more than you can see. But you can sit, turn inward and just breathe. Do this regularly, and you will perceive a whole new world.

There is no way of being more present than being present to what you are sensing at this moment, and this moment, and this moment. This process is called being mindful and is the way to train yourself out of stress and into peace. In fact, when you meditate, you will experience all of the opposite effects of stress, because meditation will put you into a state of rest where your body can automatically restore and release stored stress. Now you can feel relaxed, happy and at ease in your body, instead of feeling tension, fear, and dis-ease.

It is physically impossible for your brain to release stress chemicals and restorative chemicals at the same time. You either pump toxics or tonics, and you control the switch. How's that for empowering! The choice is yours, and there is no going back from knowing that...

So what is it that you are choosing for your body? Toxics or tonics? Are you choosing to be healthy and happy, or stressed and unwell? Every day is a new beginning. So now let's open our hearts to our bodies and all they have held for us over the years.

BODY LOVE

Our bodies store all of it's past reactions to our life's stress. Fight/flight responses create contractions, which cut us off from the expansive love energy of the Universe. Our health shows us where our body has stored stress contractions within the body, as pain, tension, and disease. We are a physical representation of our past trauma and drama.

Contraction expresses itself throughout our lives as lack of health, self-esteem, energy, money, motivation, and enthusiasm. Contraction makes us feel stuck in our lives, and in our body and turns into a block to love. Have a look around you and notice people who look like they are contracted.

Emotions show in our posture. Our body conveys how we are feeling. When we are feeling stressed, it is written on our face, and in our body language. It is evident in the way we hold our head and shoulders, and how we are breathing. A stressed mind creates a stressed body, and a stressed body creates a stressed mind, it is a never-ending story, unless we change the script. When we are relaxed and happy, others can see it on our face, and in our body language also. We look as we feel. Upright, relaxed and smiling makes us feel self-confident and energetic; while hunched, contracted and frowning makes us feel tired and depressed. Try it.

You can use this knowledge to fake it until you make it by assuming a confident, upright posture, which tells your brain that you are feeling confident and relaxed, and it will start to pump tonic chemicals. Allow yourself to feel great. Allow some space for love to grow in your body.

If you are going to ground love into Mother Earth through you, you can't vibrate anything but love for your body. To receive love to you and through you, you have to believe you deserve it, with every cell. You have to know you are good enough. You have to love your body so you can be a love revolutionary.

It sounds 'easier said than done,' as we all hold judgmental thoughts about our bodies. We never think about the good things our bodies do for us, every day without a fuss, but instead only focus on the body when things go wrong. If we could be present in the body, daily acknowledging what is going right, we could have a healthy body right now.

With a healthy body as your goal, you are going to focus yourself on all the perfect things your body does for you. Decide that you are going to love yourself exactly as you are. This decision to accept your body and love it wholeheartedly changes everything. Imagine your body learning to release its resistance to Source's pure abundance by just deciding to love yourself. That is all it takes! From here on your cells will be resonating more and more deeply in love, and the resistance in your body will melt away.

Love, acceptance, and appreciation of your body, is a lovely habit to have. Do you look after your body, or do you take it for granted and ignore it? Do you dwell on its shortcomings? Are you happy with its shape and size? Or do you bemoan your appearance? Switch that immediately! Self-criticism deflates your self-esteem like nothing else can. Focus instead on health and feeling well. Feel gratitude for all that your body is doing right, and take the spotlight off it's accused wrongs.

Decide to only speak to yourself as you would to someone you love. Your subconscious mind is listening to every word you say; *you* are listening to every word you say. So say positive, loving things. You may feel silly, and it may take some time to start to believe your talk. But in a relatively short time, you will train your thoughts to be only positive. When you catch yourself running your body down, stop and do the Switch Breath.

Challenge yourself to connect with your body and show it love every day. Find your own words and ways to tell your body how and why you love it. Shower yourself with appreciation, encourage and support your body, because someone you love - *you* - are listening to every word you say. Smile at yourself in the mirror. Look yourself in the eye and say "Hello lovely." Imagine the effect of that love after a week, a month, a year, and even a decade.

MEDITATION IS THE NEW MEDICATION

Meditation is heralded as the new medication for all that ails us. Although it feels new and is becoming popular now, it has been around for centuries, practiced within all spiritual sects.

Meditation was seen as sacred for the enlightened, to do in secrecy, usually in a cave on the very top of a mountain, or within the temples of religion. Thank goodness for these spiritual masters and all their experiences. They wrote scriptures and sutras documenting the mind and all the states of it so we can seek our own awareness using this sacred knowledge.

We live in exciting times! Science can prove now what they knew then. Numerous books have been written and are now available, which discuss the laws of quantum physics, DNA and our genes, the power of our beliefs, and the effects of our beliefs on our brains and our bodies. There has never been a better time to investigate these subjects at a deeper level.

For you to understand more about meditation, I will be sharing a simple practice that will help guide you to find acknowledgment in your humanity and spirituality, balancing both aspects as you self-love, self-heal, and self-empower. You will do this a step at a time; until you have a routine you can dance to.

As you lead up to this practice, I ask that you set aside some 'me' time to practice *meditation* daily. Acknowledge that this time is an essential part of your day. Make this a priority and watch how it positively impacts on the rest of your day. All you have to do is to decide to practice the Love Revolution. A decision is the most powerful force you have, and practice makes perfect.

Meditation enables us to consciously switch from stress mode to restoration mode, something we have forgotten how to do in our busy lives. And once we are in restoration mode, all the effects of stress we have experienced in our body and mind will begin to unravel.

Regular meditation reduces stress and anxiety, improves sleep patterns and gives us higher levels of productivity. We have the power to reverse the effects of stress and toxic chemicals, by relaxing deeply in meditation and allowing our body to restore itself and find its balance. Meditation slows aging and increases our Serotonin and Endorphin levels, which means we are calmer and happier. As you practice meditation techniques, you will find that your energy levels rise, as does your immunity and metabolism.

Also to be noted is not just the reversal effect on the brain, but the rewiring opportunity that meditation gives the brain. The brain *can* create new neural pathways. Meditation also strengthens the connection between the right and left sides of the brain, which provides us access to both when we are problem-solving and creating. We can be creative problem-solvers and logistic artists. Meditation is a brain changer!

In meditation, all boundaries vanish, and we can become aware of ourself without our body. There is a sense of coming home. We feel the merge with the Universe and feel part of the whole, we feel Oneness. We connect with divine Source energy, which brings joy, peace, and the feelings of love. Meditation is a direct pathway into the inspirational field of Source. If prayer is speaking to God, meditation is listening.

We have this incredible gift of Oneness available within all of us when we decide to step out of the busyness of the business of life and allow ourselves to sit for ten minutes. As we sit in the center of *me*, just as we are, with whatever thoughts are rolling, loving ourselves anyway, we can realize our full potential and shape our world lovingly.

Can you even imagine your full potential? Let's start right now. Find your intention, not to achieve, but to receive what is your birthright. Your power for positive change is eternally internal and eventually external. Meditation is a personal transformational process. As you discover more about yourself, you will fall in love with yourself more and more…

FIRST ADVENTURE

Unwiring your stress is the most loving thing you can do for yourself, and humanity, and is the mission of the Love Revolution. When you are stressed out, you are running on automatic pilot reacting to all that is going on around you. Meditation gives you the space and the grace to be the highest vibrating version of yourself that you can be. Miracles can, and do happen. Disease and illness can, and do, reverse. You are replacing millions of cells every minute, how cool is that?

You hold the power; all you have to do is decide to dedicate at least ten minutes a day to meditation. I know that you want to say you don't have any spare time ... but I want to tell you that you can control time, instead of time controlling you. It is only your stressed perception that is telling you to "Hurry, hurry, and get things done!"

So if your thoughts are doing that, and you feel don't have time for this life-changing ten minutes of self-care within your day, I want you to put your hand up and shout, *"Stop!"*

Create time for yourself, ten minutes, that's all. I suggest setting your alarm fifteen minutes earlier so you can get up and have a drink and a toilet visit before you sit to practice. Believe me; once you start carving ten minutes from your busy schedule and commit to yourself, you will find it easy to increase it to fifteen and maybe even twenty minutes in a very short time. You will feel the benefits of meditation immediately. And those benefits add up quickly with each session.

As muscles relax while you are sitting in meditation, they may release stored pain, just bless the pain and know it is leaving the body. As the mind relaxes, it will release stored beliefs by giving you lots to think about. Bless yourself and the lessons you have learned. Relax and continuously move towards deeper relaxation.

The decision to join the Love Revolution is one that your soul has long been waiting for. It is the journey from being dependent on others for our expansion, to becoming only dependent on ourselves. It is about being your own Guru. **G**ee, yo**U** a**R**e yo**U**! This process will allow you to experience expansion within your being and even more divine, you will experience who you truly are. That is love.

Once you commit to the practice, proceed slowly and surely through each step, gaining confidence as you go. You deserve the time and space to allow yourself to flourish. If you rush through the process, you will miss the most important lesson, which is to *be here now*, and it will mean that you will not get to ground the work.

So here is your first intrepid adventure, simply find a comfortable seat and make the conscious decision to meditate. Read through these instructions, and then go ahead and give it a go. I suggest you read before meditating for the next few days, as you learn the routine. You don't have to get it right, and you can't get it wrong.

Do not be tempted to hurry through the steps, as they are a systematic process to deepen and strengthen your practice steadily. Go too fast, and you will not reap the benefits that this practice offers you. The Love Revolution needs strong leaders, so take the time to strengthen you.

PRACTICE

This first meditation will transition your body and mind from busy to still. You will sit within your body and just *be*. You will first connect to Mother Earth, to ground you in this journey. Being grounded allows you to feel safe and nurtured as Mother Earth can hold your space, while you drop your full weight onto her. To be safe when you fly high you need to feel anchored, and this step allows you to feel just that.

Find a comfortable seat, on a cushion or a chair. Do not lie down as you will invite sleep, which is fine if that is what you are after, but sleep is not meditation. Sit in an upright position with an unsupported head; this will mean if you 'nod off,' your head nodding will bring you back into your meditative state. It is a fine line for a beginner, so welcome the feeling of deep comfort, and nod off if you have to, but when you become aware again, simply return to the meditation.

Make sure you will not be interrupted, there is nothing quite like snapping out of a meditative state to the sound of the telephone, or someone suddenly entering the room you are sitting in. Tell those you live with that you are meditating and want to be undisturbed for a while, and turn your phone off.

It is okay that the rest of the house goes about their business without tiptoeing, as it is important that you learn to meditate within everyday situations. Let's not be precious about this; let's make this as normal as can be.

If you have a busy mind, you could have a pad and a pen ready to jot down anything that seems necessary, or you could be lucky enough to receive flashes of insight and inspiration. Lots of answers to tricky problems come in the mental silence of meditation.

Always start with the Switch Breath, as it is a reset before you meditate.

Begin breathing in for four, hold for four, out for four, hold for four. Do this complete round four times, and then let the breath return to its natural rhythm. Slowly shut your eyes, if they aren't already, and sit for a few breaths feeling into the body. Listen to the noises around you.

Start a slow scan of the body, starting at the head and moving down to the toes. Notice the big spaces like shoulders and legs, and notice the small spaces like fingers and toes. Allow your mind to travel through the body, connecting to all. Don't analyze the body, just notice where you are holding tension and allow yourself to relax. Wiggle, jiggle and move towards comfort. Keep the mind passively on task, checking in with the body and finding deeper comfort.

Once you have completed the body scan, place your hand on your belly and allow your awareness to move there. Tune into your belly and feel the flow of energy there. Focus only on the space in your belly, and the movement of the breath there. Once you are connected to the belly, you can return your hand to your resting position.

Feel the expansion and the contraction of the breath in the belly, the in and out, the ebb and flow. Mentally watch the breath, and feel into it. Allow your mind to drop deep into the body and feel the body to move into relaxation, sinking into itself. Feel deeply comfortable in the body and more toward deeper comfort.

Watch the breath and notice the energy moves up into the belly when the breath moves down into it. And when you exhale the breath moves up, and the energy moves down. Spend some time feeling into the expansion and contraction of this. Air flows in and down; energy flows in and up. Air flows up and out, energy flows down and out.

You are just sitting and witnessing, and settling deeper.

Start to feel that as you inhale that you are breathing in from the heart of Mother Earth, and as you exhale you are sinking deeper into that sacred space. Bring your awareness to Mother Earth and feel your connection to the floor.

Feel the energy moving up and down from the heart of Mother Earth, grounding you, holding you, keeping you safe. You are going to allow yourself to grow roots deep into her heart, to receive her support, just like a mother.

Now you have allowed the body to settle, and you are connected to the very heart of the Mother Earth, you can now give the mind something to do.

Counting the breaths, one to ten, again and again. Counting up to ten gives the mind a long leash to wander, so you aren't forcing the mind to calm, you are giving it space to unravel if it has to. If you catch yourself past the number ten, and you will, just kindly and without judgment bring yourself back to one and start again.

Inhale to one
Exhale to two
Inhale to three
Exhale to four...
and so on to ten.

Meditation brings you to the *now* moment. Just watching the belly moving, counting the breaths, bringing your awareness back to now... now... now... now... and the thoughts will naturally wind down.

When you find a thought, I want you to acknowledge it, and then take the mind back to one. One to ten, again and again. The mind likes to think, so let thoughts come and go, but train it to focus on the numbers of the count.

One to ten, again, and again, and again.

Stay with this for a few minutes, until the mind has settled into the routine of the count and has stopped trying to distract you. Then you can allow the count to stop and rest. Feel the support of Mother Earth. Be peaceful with whatever this space is for you today. Each day will be different.

When you feel complete, bring yourself back to noises outside the body, back to the noises of the world around you. Keeping your eyes closed, become aware of the body sitting. Become aware of the space around you, and you in the space. Take as long as you can to come back, the longer you take, the more tonics you bring with you. Become aware of your fingers and toes, and wiggle them. Stretch, and move slowly back to reality.

Once you feel ready, open your eyes slowly and look around you. See things with your new relaxed and clear vision, and enjoy your new perspective. When you are ready to get up, do it with the intention to go forth into your day with your new attitude.

Congratulations! You have completed your first adventure. Practice this for a week until you can slip in and out of this body space easily... and then read on.

3

CROWN YOURSELF IN LOVE

HEAD SPACE

Now WE ARE SAFELY rooted in Mother Earth, we are going to explore our head space, which houses our brain, our mind, and is where we connect spiritually to divine Source/God force. There is a lot of energy to be received through our crown chakra, on the top of our head, and there is a lot of activity continually going on in our mind and within our brain.

We actually could say we have three brains operating within our heads, each with their own circuitry and chemistry, which move us through the stages of *think*ing in the Neo Cortex, *feel*ing in the Limbic and *be*ing in the Cerebellum. The Neo

Cortex is the outside cap that we are used to seeing as an image of the brain, and it is where thought happens. The Limbic Brain is a smaller part within the brain, which we use for learning and memory, and it is where our emotions originate. The Cerebellum is smaller again but has the most significant hold on us as it is wired up for survival and controls the fight/flight response.

Neo Cortex, the thinking cap, creates new connections within the brain every time we experience something new. Each time we think a new thought our brain reorganizes itself, and we 'change our mind.' This process brings an emotional response and our Limbic brain releases the appropriate chemicals, and then stores that response as a memory. Meanwhile, the Cerebellum brain is forever on standby, prepared to save us in stressful situations.

These three brains are continually moving through the dance of perception and response. They are reacting to what is going on outside us, as reality, and what is going on inside of us as memories. All of our memories are stored in our brain, good and bad. Every time we remember something we get a flood of the chemicals associated with that time, which is great if our memory is happy. But if our memory is fear based we will flood our system with toxic chemicals, which then signals the Cerebellum to engage the fight/flight response as we remember. Where we attention goes, energy flows.

This constant process of thinking, feeling, and being is what creates our personality, our ego. Ego is an intelligence that is acquired through our lifetime, and it has worked to keep us safe and alive. Ego is based on the decisions we make about ourselves, and the world around us. Most of these decisions have come from the experiences we had as a child and the way we were brought up within our family. The stories we perceive as children become the stories we receive as adults and most of our decisions about ourselves are made before the age of seven. You can recognize what decisions you have made by listening to the stories you tell yourselves, and others.

All these decisions carry chemicals through the body, and the brain finds a set point, which it considers normal. As an adult, the brain is still responding to this set point from childhood, which influences how we feel about ourselves, and how we view the world around us. It also gives us automatic responses to stress, which is why most adults behave like children in stressful situations. It is all coming from the subconscious, from our programming.

Most of these decisions come from a universal need to belong. We tend to hide our true selves in an attempt to conform to our family and society. As children, we are empathically finding ways to belong, and we change our behaviors to fit in. We make decisions based on whom we think we 'should be' and behave accordingly.

The energy of 'should' carries the emotional imprints of shame and guilt, which gives us anxiety and causes stress within the body. Shame makes us withdraw into ourselves, and when we do venture out, we do it by wanting to please or appease others. Guilt is shame felt for the way we have behaved. 'Should' also causes procrastination, which is a crippling, self-imposed, web of resistance. All of this 'shoulding' is stressful and has an impact on our body, mind, and life as we suppress who we 'really' are and start knee-jerking through life.

Trying to fit into a preconceived notion of what is right and what is wrong leaves many of us struggling with ourselves. Our goal becomes to fit in, and we do this by seeking approval outside of ourselves and this, of course, amplifies our feelings of being on the outer. Pleasing and appeasing becomes a habitual pattern.

How can we know who we are when we are constantly comparing ourselves to others? How can we have inner peace when we are so busy looking outward for connection and approval? We are a generation of self-suppressors. We are numbing ourselves. Let's stop that now! Let's look at our mind...

IN TWO MINDS

Our head space also houses the mind, divided into the conscious and the subconscious. According to ancient spiritual texts, the seat of the mind is in the pituitary gland and the pineal gland, which reside in the middle of the brain. These master glands are a part of the endocrine system and help control many functions within the body. The pituitary gland is known as the seat of the conscious mind, while the pineal gland is known as the seat of the subconscious mind.

The pituitary is masculine and is a transmitter sending signals to control all other glands and organs within the body. The pineal is feminine and is a receiver, also known as the seat of the Third Eye, from which we connect to the spiritual realms. The pineal receives impressions and information from the outer world, which we then base our daily lives on. It is interesting to note that the pineal, the receiver, sits behind the pituitary, the transmitter. Literally, our wisdom sits behind our thinking.

It is said that we have two minds. The conscious mind, with its constant outward flow of thought, is the part of us that is tuned into fear, and expectation and is constantly transmitting 'who I am' out into the world. It is also projecting our perceptions onto others around us, as a way to keep us safe. It is our conscious mind that decides who we are, and how to be. It is logical and structured.

The subconscious mind with its constant inward flow of receiving is connected to the Source energy of the Universe and is the part of us that is tuned into emotions, creativity, inspiration, intuition, and beliefs.

It is the conscious mind that thinks a thought repeatedly until it turns into a belief in the subconscious. The thought is transmitted it as a frequency, from the pituitary. The subconscious then receives what it believes to be true from Source energy, via the pineal. We are thinking and perceiving, believing and receiving. That's it!

We could look at it like this… We decide to purchase some music online, so we select an album and transmit a request for an MP3 to the source in the clouds, and then we receive a download of what we requested. Our conscious mind makes a decision and the subconscious mind tunes into and receives from Source. We receive what we think about.

To achieve personal growth, the best thing we can do is to learn how the conscious and the subconscious mind work together, and then take advantage of their combined force.

The conscious mind uses around 5% of our total mind, to think and analyze. It is this part of the mind which responds to our physical senses, which is how we experience the physical world around us. It is, most importantly, the conscious mind that can reason. This skill sets us apart from other animals, as we can make decisions consciously, and therefore shape our lives. Our ability to direct our attention is a power we use every day. When we decide to do something with awareness, we are using our conscious mind.

The subconscious mind is the remaining 95% and is in control of our spiritual connection, intuition, creativity, emotions, beliefs, relationship patterns, habits and addictions and our long-term memory. Our subconscious mind is infinitely more powerful than the conscious mind. And though we do use our subconscious mind in a lot of ways, we don't use it consciously.

Our conscious mind is in control of our daily life, but it is our subconscious that holds the key to our future life. The subconscious mind does not think or reason; it merely obeys orders it receives from your conscious mind. Our conscious mind talks away all day, and our subconscious mind delivers to us what we are thinking about. The subconscious mind is a servant who always says "Yes" and is always giving us what we ask for, whether we actually want it or not. Whether it is a blessing or a stressing. The choice is always ours. Remember, where attention goes, energy flows.

Think of the conscious mind as a gardener, planting seeds in the extremely fertile soil of the subconscious. If we plant vegetable seeds, we get vegetables. If we plant flower seeds, we get flowers. And if we plant weed seeds, we will get weeds. We reap what we sow. The soil does not decide what to grow, we the gardener does. Just like the subconscious mind does not decide what to grow, the conscious mind does.

The subconscious mind will manifest out of love or fear, with no preference. Love and fear will show up in our life as abundance or lack, health or disease, success or failure. Whatever we repeatedly think about, with emotion, the subconscious will produce in our life. The garden is watered, and blessed from the Universe, weeds, vegetables and prize roses alike.

We all want to live in love, but we are mostly living in fear. Fear of failure, abandonment, rejection, criticism, and judgment. We are light-seeking beings, who unfortunately get lost in the shadows of our negative emotions, which are yet to have a light shone on them. We get crippled by our issues, our dramas, and our traumas. We can lose control of our emotions and act in ways we wish we didn't, remember this is when we need some love, yet this is also when we feel unworthy of it. We believe we just aren't good enough to step out of the shadows and into the light of love.

Behaviors and habits that we don't like about ourselves are hidden in our subconscious and are known as our Shadow. It is our Shadow that is our dark side. But remember there cannot be light without dark, and there cannot be dark without light. Light and dark are both necessary for our personal growth. When we don't look at and accept our Shadow, we tend to project our stuff onto others. Accepting our Shadow requires us to witness our thoughts. Only then can we get a clearer understanding of what we believe.

We all inhabit the world, with our Shadows acting out unconsciously through our personalities. Look around and notice that it's not just you who hides in the shadows. We all do! We all have negative subconscious patterns running from the decisions we made as children to survive humanity, and fit in. We all have 'stuff' we would rather keep in the shadows. We connect to each other from this shadow space. We are all reacting and responding to each other's Shadows.

We live in a time where we are always connected to the world wide web of instant communication. Social media gives us access to each other everywhere we go through our mobile phones. Emails, online searches, texting, social media sites are all in our pocket. We can spend hours, and many of us do, checking in to what the rest of humanity is doing, and reacting to that. We are all looking for instant gratification through instant communication, and have other people's thoughts and opinions flying around us constantly. We are a generation that looks outwards for stimulation and connection. We are brainwashing our subconscious with outside influences. How about we brainwash our subconscious with inside influences?

CHANGE YOUR MIND

Spiritual teachings all agree that we create our world from the inside out. Our perceptions create our reality, so if we choose to perceive fear, we will see only that, and live in a world full of fear and anger. If we choose to perceive love, then that is what we see, and we will live in a world full of love. It sounds simple, and it is.

To be aware of the power of perception is liberating as we can begin to shape our lives, by changing our perceptions. We can take back the reins of our destiny. We can live to our full potential. And how do we change our perceptions? By understanding how the conscious mind and the subconscious mind work together, and using their combined power to affect our lives.

We can begin to change our mind, and then watch our mind change the shape and the style of our world around us.

95% of what we think, say and do comes from the subconscious, in the form of habitual thoughts and actions. The conscious mind is only in charge 5% of the time. By understanding the balance of power within the mind, and the power of the conscious mind to imprint on the subconscious mind, we can see the importance of being very careful about what we think. We need to get conscious about our subconscious.

The subconscious mind is easily influenced and is always watching and listening, especially to background noises like other's opinions, books, television and radio. If we do not run our subconscious mind, outside influences will. The subconscious is easily brainwashed. A frightening thought, but a good one to know, because we can take advantage of this trait. You are going to practice brainwashing yourself. "I love myself!" Repeat, repeat, and repeat…

Repetition creates new beliefs in the subconscious mind. Think or say anything enough and you will begin to believe it, even if it is imagined. Further to this the subconscious files memories as mental movies, complete with the emotional data. It doesn't have any perception of time, past or future; it is only in the *now*. The subconscious mind has no opinion. It is like a computer that stores what you put in, and that can come from either your imagination or your reality.

Be aware of how thoughts affect your circumstances; pay much attention to what you are thinking. By acknowledging your thoughts are the creative energy in your life, and becoming responsible for what you think, you can start to change your mind, and your life. The conscious mind is the master, and the subconscious mind is the obedient servant that always says "Yes!"

Remember, the subconscious mind is the keeper of your memories, and you have to access the emotions within the memory banks of the subconscious mind to make any positive changes. It is the emotional energy, which is the magic ingredient. That is why affirmations can seem so senseless and can have no effect. Affirmations done with the conscious mind, and without the connection to the memory bank in the subconscious, can become a massive waste of time. You have to connect your affirmation "I love myself!" with some emotional memory. You have to consciously decide to accept it and then think about corresponding memories to match it.

Stop reading and close your eyes, take a Switch Breath and relax. I want you to remember a time where you felt love, from another human or even a pet. Replay the scene with as much detail as you can. Watch the mental movie and feel the emotions, feel the subconscious at work.

Now imagine standing with your arms open, feeling that love. Tune it in as finely as you can, and turn it up. Access that same emotion you have already found. Let those emotions flood you. Put as much detail into your movie as you can find. Use all the senses, what can you see, smell, touch, taste and how do you feel? Use your imagination to create, direct, and produce your movie. See yourself full of love, relaxed and confident. Notice the glow that emanates from you and the smile that you wear. Feel your cells buzzing with love, warm fuzzies bubbling through your body. Tune it in and turn it up again. Hold this vision for at least a minute, allowing the energy to grow and glow brighter.

This process is using your conscious mind to make decisions about what scene you want, and how you want to feel within it. The conscious mind becomes the director, and you as the lead actor need to practice the lines and the emotions necessary to portray your role. Feel the joy in your heart, see yourself standing tall and strong, smile and action! Repeat to you, and to the Universe, "I love myself!"

"I love myself!" unlocks all of the goodness in the Universe. Love is the pure abundance of Universal energy. "I love myself!" opens the gates to love, health, happiness, beauty, self-confidence, success, prosperity … the list goes on. You will be healthy, wealthy and wise. You will begin to attract, at a quantum level, situations and people that match your love vibration. You will know that your Love Revolution has indeed started.

SOURCE ENERGY

Science shows us that everything is energy and that energy makes everything, including ourselves. We have a physical body that moves in this world of matter, and we have an energetic body, which moves in a subtler world.

Source energy has a high frequency and emanates from the center of our Earth's Universe. It is this energy that flows to, and through us all. Source energy is what we breathe. We fill ourselves up with every inhale we take. Source fuels us; it is the elixir of life. Positive emotions vibrate towards the high frequency being transmitted from the Universe as Source energy. Negative emotions cause resistance to receiving Source energy.

Think of the word emotion, e-motion = energy in motion. Think how low frequency, negative emotions like resentment, anger, hatred, and grief affect the body. You can see stress embodied in people around you, and also within yourself. Now imagine how high frequency, positive emotions can also affect the body. Love, happiness, peace, contentment, joy, gratitude...

When you have emotions that feel good, you are vibrating up towards Source, and when you have emotions that feel bad, you are resisting the flow of Source. You can connect to Source energy as a happy soul and create new exciting times; or you can connect as a victim and create old miserable times. The way to know how much Source energy you are allowing is to be aware of your emotions.

The aim is for you to know what you are asking for, of what you are transmitting. Are you worrying? It will only invite more of what you are worried about. Are you jealous? Are you thinking, "They have what I don't!" If so you will only receive more lack. Are you focused on pain? "Yes!" says the Universe, have some more of that. Are you feeling depressed? Resentful? Angry? Overwhelmed? Become aware of what you are asking the Universe to give you.

When you catch a negative frequency, pause and practice the Switch Breath. You are becoming conscious, and are claiming your power, which is releasing you from old patterns. This process requires you to feel low emotions and to confirm that you love yourself, when you need it most. It will take practice. Stick with it and see where it goes.

Love is everywhere. It is the nature of the Universe, and it is the true nature of us all. It may appear that we are all joined in war and fear and hate, but that is just the active ego energy on the planet. Fear, in usual ego fashion, loves the drama and the spotlight. It loves distracting others from seeing the love. Fear is like a virus, and it spreads fast, as people entrain to it.

But love has a higher vibration and therefore a stronger influence. Everything rises to love, once we stop blocking it and holding it down. Imagine a world full of love, a world free of fear. It is a seemingly impossible vision. If we can focus on loving ourselves and spreading our vibration from there, we make a significant impact on the planet. By loving ourselves and allowing ourselves to overflow with love, we express compassion and unconditional love to others around us also.

You can decide *now* to allow your cells to reach their full potential, by tuning them into the frequency of love. Connect with your highest possible vibration, and fill yourself up to overflowing. Stand tall as a love revolutionary and ground it down into Mother Earth. Grow roots through your boots, deep into the divine heart of the Mother. Be the anchor of love, and your cells will light up. You will light up!

Allow yourself to forgive. Bury that hatchet and smoke that peace pipe. Allow yourself to let go of past hurts and grudges. Allow yourself to step into your full potential. Decide it, and take your power back.

By feeling into love, and practicing how it feels, you can start to move out of fear. You can vibrate above it; you can feel 'over it.' If love is the strongest request, then the brain will release negative, fearful connections. The memories of worry, anger, and stress around a situation will fade, and those neural connections will let go and begin to connect in a new way. You have to practice and repeat, repeat, repeat until you do not have to think about it, and then it becomes a new way of being. Now you are love. Now you are changing your cells, and now you are transmitting love from a cellular level.

SECOND ADVENTURE

In the last chapter, you examined your body space and started your meditation practice. You grounded your stress and rooted deeply into Mother Earth, and now you are going to connect to divine Source energy from above, through your head space.

As above, so below.

Some days aren't peaceful when you are sitting in meditation. Some days are far from peaceful, and you may notice discomfort emotionally or physically. Do not suppress anything. Let stuff come up, and then move towards deeper comfort. Allow what wants to be expressed, space and time to show itself. Don't rush this step, it may seem boring, but the longer you spend getting settled and comfortable, the longer you will be able to sit. You are creating a strong foundation for the rest of your meditation practice.

If your body twitches, rocks, jolts or shudders, you are releasing stress and trauma, therefore relaxing into deeper comfort. You might even feel a pain appear in the body. As you focus on the pain it may feel overpowering; it may feel like it is growing. Acknowledge the pain, and move towards deeper comfort. You could place your hand on the painful area. Hold the pain, hold the space for the pain, and continue with your meditation.

Let things rise and release. Do not pay any attention to what is coming up and just allow it to pass through. By doing this, you tell your subconscious that it isn't important, and the subconscious will release it. Witness what is happening within the body, and the mind then accepts it is as it is, without judgment and expectation.

With that surrendered attitude, you will relax further; you will find the gap between the thoughts and maybe even fall into the gap between the thoughts. And that my friend is meditation! Falling into the gap, bouncing out again, lovingly accepting that. Bringing yourself lovingly back to now, and falling into the gap again. That's it, that's the secret. Just sitting and being, accepting and loving.

Some days you will fall into the gap easily, some days you may sit for 15 minutes feeling teased by the very notion of it. Some days old 'stuff' may arise, just welcome it and keep breathing. Let things arise and release, do not pay attention and flow energy there. Just allow and show your mind that it is no longer important, and your mind will release it.

Feel acceptance and love for that which is showing up to be seen. Meditation trains you to sit and witness. Simply accept and be happy with whatever your meditation is for you today. Allow yourself to just sit, with no expectations, and let the mind do what it wants. If it wants to show you visions, allow it. If it wants to think, allow it. If it wants to release old drama, allow it. If it wants to rest, allow it. Let it be. Do not oppress yourself. This is the path to enlightenment.

Over the centuries enlightened beings have been painted with a halo above their heads. A halo is a lovely image for us, but I prefer to see it as a crown, gifted to us from the Universe. A crown of spiritual grace, a symbol of the power you have over your life. The monarch of your destiny, the ruler of your world and the master of your life.

Now let's continue on our journey and plug into the Universe to crown ourselves, as we move into the next stage of the meditation.

PRACTICE

Find your seat and begin with the Switch Breath, and then proceed through the scan of the body, the connection to Mother Earth and the counting. One to ten, again and again. Once the mind has settled and is counting without interruption, we can then move on to the head space.

We are going to assume as truth, because it is, that the flow of energy we have established with the breath from the belly of Mother Earth is still flowing, and now we are going to establish a connection to Source.

Place your hand on your head and connect there. Focus on your head space. Watch the breath move in and out of the head space. Feel the expansion and the contraction of the head space. Return your hand to your lap once you have a strong connection.

Start allowing the energy of the breath to move in and out of the top of the head. See yourself with a beautiful crown on, and the energy pouring through it like a funnel into your skull.

Notice that the breath is flowing up from Mother Earth, and meeting the breath from Source in your heart space. Mixing and mingling. Flowing in and out from both ends of your being.

Focus on the divine Source energy flowing in with your breath, through your crown and into your body. Feel your connection to the Universe. See this energy as healing light, which is filling you up. Allow this beautiful light to spread into every nook and cranny, every cell within you. Light up your cells. Breathe light in, feel it circulating, and breathe light out. Don't get hung up on what color the light is… just notice and promise yourself that you will think about it later… and breathe.

Don't let the mind start to distract you, stay as blank as you can. As you practice this step over the next week, you will find that your mind will learn just to sit and watch the light. Open yourself to divine love. Let it in. Receive and feel the bliss of it. Get your glow on! Crown yourself with light.

Be aware of inspired thoughts coming to you, thoughts from the Universe, thoughts you are not thinking. Let these flashes of inspiration come and go. Easy come and easy go. No judgment or expectation, just relaxing by moving into deeper comfort and receiving. Just being crowned in love.

Sit and receive for as long as you can, enjoy the experience. Then when you are ready, allow yourself to become more aware of noises. Start to tune yourself to the outside world. Slowly come back and stretch. Continue with your day, and don't forget your crown.

Again, practice the Switch Breath, Body Space and Head Space for a week, and then continue on.

Express Yourself In Love

HEART SPACE

Welcome to the heart space, the home of our emotional body, and of our heart's desires. It is where we are either open or closed to love and support, from humans and the spiritual realm. The heart space is in the middle of the body and is the meeting place of earth energy with spiritual energy, which means we can be grounded in the realm of the physical, flying high with inspiration from the spiritual realms, and expressing ourselves to the world through our heart.

Healthy physical hearts open and shut, and our emotional heart should open and shut too. There is a natural balance to that.

There is also a natural rhythm to the heart, and a natural speed. When we are stressed, our heart is beating faster and therefore upsetting its natural rhythm. Our heart rate and our emotions are linked, and therefore so are our chemical responses, toxic or tonic. When we feel frustrated, impatient, irritated or hurried, our heart rhythm speeds up and becomes irregular, which signals the brain to pump fight/flight chemicals.

When we feel relaxed, happy, gratitude, compassion or love, our heart rhythm slows to a more settled pattern, which signals the brain to pump restorative chemicals, which calms the mind and the body further, which makes more tonics flow. When our heart and biochemical systems are working together at an optimum level, it is called coherence.

Science has proven that the heart has its own brain with its own network of receptors and transmitters. The heart also has tissue similar to the brain. A crucial role of the heart's brain is to monitor chemical changes within the body, by assessing emotions and converting them to electrical impulses to tell the brain to correct the levels. Every decision our brain makes comes from the heart.

The heart is also more energetic than our brain, being the strongest generator of magnetic and electrical fields. Stronger than the brain! This means that the space of our emotional body has more power than our mental body. When we have a feeling in the heart, we produce electrical and magnetic energy that can interrupt and actually change the pattern of the energy around us. By giving and receiving love, we help others physically, mentally and emotionally. Love is the greatest healer.

Spiritual texts agree that the power of humanity lies outside the mind, and in the heart. They talk about accessing the heart's ability for self-healing and intuition. If we accept that the heart is not only a powerful pump but also an organ of perception and wisdom, we can embrace the heart and all of its gifts.

It is through our heart space that we feel our connection to the world, or not. Either way, we are emphasizing and reinforcing what we feel, positive or negative. We are also connecting with other people's hearts, again positively or negatively. Awareness of this gives us the opportunity to set a high vibration radiating from our heart; with the scientific knowledge that another's heart will rise to meet yours.

We are empathic beings, which means we feel with our heart and entrain our energy to match what we are observing. Be careful of being empathic though, as we can take on the symptoms and pain of others. Empathy means, "I feel your pain," and compassion means, "I see your pain, and I honor your life."

By feeling another's pain, we climb down into their despair, and then we are there with them, supporting them in the dark. By tuning ourselves up to compassion, we are still supporting them, but we are not going down to them. We are staying in our lighter state, and only light can conquer the dark. We can hold a higher frequency which invites their energy to entrain up to ours, making their journey their own. We are not rescuing or pulling others up; we are smiling from our compassionate viewpoint and showing them that we believe in them.

It is so much more loving to you, and others, to feel compassion. It is an act of loving self-care, and it is showing respect for another's path. Best not to worry. Leave the rest of humanity to their journey and only focus on your own. Remember their business is not your business. You do not need to understand why or how others are experiencing life. You need to be above that. You need to overstand, not understand.

The reason to worry may be valid, but at this moment, you are only imagining, and imagination creates your future. You will start making mountains out of molehills. Cross that bridge when you get to it, do not live in a state of always expecting the worst. Worrying about something is projecting fear into the future. Worrying about someone is projecting fear onto them. A conscious practice is to do the Switch Breath whenever you find yourself worrying, and then send them some love.

I would like to unravel empathy a little further. I hear the statement "I picked up another's pain," a lot in my work, and I am daring you to dive deeper into that. Sit for a moment and feel into another's pain, and then ask yourself "Is that their pain I am feeling?" The answer is "No!" It can only be your pain you are feeling.

As you perceive and assume their pain, you are assuming the feelings of what you are perceiving. You assume you know how it feels. But as much as you *think* you understand how someone may be feeling, you cannot *know* how another is feeling. You are feeling your own pain, which resonates with theirs. You are feeling triggered, but not owning it and therefore projecting it onto them. So please do not assume you are feeling another's pain. It just doesn't work like that.

If you feel triggered by any outside event, be it close to home or outside, like on the television; stop and do the Switch Breath. Switch from fear to love.

We are now acutely aware of what is happening on the planet. The World Wide Web tells us everything we want to know and lots of things we don't. Even with all our differences, we all want a peaceful planet. We want conscious evolved leaders. We want safe communities to live in. We want answers to poverty and the greenhouse effect. We want physical, mental and emotional health. We want freedom from limitations. We want to be off our medications. We want to be more conscious and aware. We all want love.

RELATIONSHIPS

Love makes the world go around, and relationships are the world trips we take. But what is love? What a tricky question, as it is often the absence of love that we are most aware of. Unfortunately, love has a lot of judgments and expectations placed on it. Questions are continually asked, "Does he love me?" "Does she love me?" "Am I loved?" "Am I lovable?"

It is enough to do your head in and to close your heart. We look for love within our relationships, our family and our friends, and within romance. But relationships keep us outwardly focused on the 'other' in the relationship, by always seeking approval and continuously questioning ourselves. A relationship is always about the two. Fear is about the two as well. Me and you, us and them, victims and villains. Gone is the Oneness, the very essence of love.

When we fall in love with another, we have a heightened emotional and chemical reaction in our system. We experience a high, which is lovingly called the 'honeymoon phase.' We become hooked to being loved and being in love, and we believe that the other person is the source of our feelings, which can only lead to unfulfilled expectations and dissatisfaction within the relationship.

But a relationship is the fastest way to get to know *you*. There is no greater growth opportunity than in a relationship, where your partner is your mirror. Most of our issues are within relationships. And just as the relationship is a healing opportunity for you, it is also a healing opportunity for the other within it.

When we love someone, the best thing we can do for them is to be happy and stable within ourselves. When we are not, and then expect the other to fix us, we are expecting the impossible. Nobody else can fix our lack of love; only we can do that.

Love and the sense of belonging are the two primary human needs. We are all yearning for love and connection, but we usually don't understand what true love really is. Ancestral wounds passed down from generation to generation means that our relationships are generally co-dependent. 'My inner child and your inner child recognize each other and want to play.'

We end up attracting matching pieces to ours and can find ourselves in a relationship where neither participant knows what healthy love is. There is a tug of war, a push and pull between clingy and detached, needy and aloof, control and rebel. Unfortunately, neediness in one causes more aloofness in the other, which causes more neediness.

So it goes, around and around, triggering our inner child, who seeks relief by triggering the other. The prevailing self-limiting belief is 'I am not good enough.' Until we clear this old belief, we will forever be stuck in this pattern, as our wounds will surface time and again within relationships.

Imagine the benefits once you switch from focusing on the other, and practice self-love. The benefits will show in all of your other relationships too, because the more you can give love to yourself, the more you can receive love from others. I'll say that another way. The amount of love you can receive outwardly equals the amount you can receive inwardly. And again, you can only feel love as deeply as the love you hold for yourself.

And loving another? You can only ever give what you already have. To give love, you must have love. To have love, you've got to love yourself. Only then can you love others in the true spirit of love. It seems so obvious, but so many of us are giving love to others, without first giving love to ourselves. No wonder we get exhausted with loving and relationships die. So, give the love you long to experience, to yourself first and foremost! And like magic, your relationships will begin to transform. Then you will be truly loved.

Loving yourself shows others how to treat you. It shows the world energetically that you value yourself. It is showing the Universe that you are worthy of love. Not because of what you look like, or what you have achieved, but simply because love is every human's birthright, no matter what.

So, continue to fill yourself up with love. Continue to state, "I love myself!" Keep your love tank full, so you don't ever feel depleted. Fill yourself up with love, and then overflow it to others, and then go and fill yourself up again.

Don't worry about what others think or say about you. Don't take anything personally! You are the only one who matters. What others think and say is just a reflection of where they are at, in that moment. It is not about you; it is never about you. It is all about them. You create what you think about, and they do too. So only ever focus on what you are thinking and saying about you.

Keep smiling at your partner, your family, and your friends, and know that the clearer you get, the clearer they can see you. Let Others Voluntarily Evolve. Never try to force love on anyone. Gift love, and then leave them to do with it what they choose. Only ever be concerned about how you are receiving love.

You will find your life changing around you, as you gain clarity on yourself. You are experiencing a significant tune-up, and some things will not resonate with you anymore. Relationships and situations are shape-shifting and redefining around you. People and situations will either tune-up to you or shake/take themselves out. As upsetting as that can be in the moment, in hindsight, it is always a good thing. Change is OK!

BE THE CHANGE YOU WANT TO SEE

When you change how you think, you change how you feel and therefore how you act. When you change how you act, you start to change your world around you. You will live your life with a new attitude, view your life with a new perspective, and now you can make new decisions within your daily life. You have climbed out of your old thinking rut and are revolutionizing your life. You can now decide to allow yourself to become who you really are.

To express love is to be the change you want to see. If you want better health, love your body. If you want better wealth, love your money. If you want a better job, love the one you have. Where ever you want to see change is precisely where you have to throw some love. Love cures all.

There is a special magic about loving where you are and what you have got, as it opens up the door for the Universe to supply you with more things for you to love. If you can vibrate love as your expression to the Universe, the Universe will always broadcast love right back to you. This reflected energy of love builds on itself, forever growing stronger, continually giving you what you love, or something better. Now you are creating a new story.

Keep focused on the story you want to create and hold it dear to your heart. Guard it preciously. Think only lovely thoughts, speak only lovely words and act lovingly - or not at all. Don't forget that where attention goes, energy flows. Always do your best within each day, and do not judge yourself harshly. Had a bad day? Love yourself back into love. Always appreciate your journey and how far you have come.

Develop an attitude of gratitude. Science has proven that 10 minutes of feeling gratitude is long enough to pump a potent chemical throughout our body, which is our most potent defense against bacteria and viruses. How fabulous is that? As well as keeping us well, gratitude also increases sleep and decreases depression. It deepens our relationships, makes us more optimistic and gives us resilience when life throws us a hurdle. Gratitude is saying "Yes!" to *all* of your life and everything in it. There is a whole lot less to stress about when you can count your blessings.

Play the gratitude game. Be thankful for every, and anything. Challenge yourself to find gratitude even when it is seemingly impossible. Thank your car, even if it is getting old and unreliable; open yourself up to receive a new car. Thank your body for the many ways it functions perfectly in your day, even if it is sore or unwell, and open yourself up for better health. Thank your mind for showing you what is still lurking in the shadows, open yourself up to more clarity.

If you practice gratitude for 10 minutes, you are not only pumping those bug-killing chemicals, but you are also projecting your desire for more to be grateful for to come into your life. "More of this, or something better." A grateful heart is a magic magnet for miracles. I recommend a daily gratitude practice of writing in a journal. Writing helps to ground gratitude through you, and down into Mother Earth.

Fill yourself up with gratitude, and overflow it around you. The more you talk about and feel gratitude, the more your subconscious mind says "Yes Master!" Remember that the subconscious mind's job description is to fetch evidence from the Universe of what you are thinking and talking about. The frequency you send out is the frequency you match and dictates the flow of Source energy you allow yourself to receive. Gratitude and appreciation are right at the top of the frequency scale. Be thankful for anything and everything, and the Universe will match that vibration and give you more. Use the conscious mind to transmit gratitude and appreciation towards the future. Celebrate your blessings and appreciate your life every day.

Make 'thank you' a mantra. See how many times you can say, "Thank you!" to others around you during your day. Show gratitude for all they are. Say, "Thank you!" to your pets too; they will receive the energetic transmission of this. Look in the mirror and say, "Thank you!" to the being reflected there.

Show gratitude to yourself, especially on bad days. Be grateful for the things that trigger and challenge you. Appreciate any opportunity to realign yourself. Celebrate that stashed trash is being detoxed from your cellular memory. If something arises emotionally, just remember that your cells are already clearing it and have brought it to your awareness. Fabulous! That's something to be grateful for! And with all this gratitude flowing, you can then soften into forgiveness.

Forgive yourself and your wrongs, because with forgiveness comes love. The burden of unforgiven situations chain us, cripple us in fear, and destroy our life over and over. Forgiveness means letting go of the whole situation and all our thoughts on the situation. I am not asking you to forgive others for the unforgivable. Some things cannot be forgiven. But, you can always forgive yourself for being the victim in the situation.

Self-forgiveness is the first step, in fact, a vast leap, towards self-love. Let it go! Do it for you, because you love yourself. Do it for your peace of mind. Do it for your health. All disease comes from resistance to love, so if you are feeling unwell, I suggest you look around to see whom and what you can forgive. The one you find hardest to forgive is the one who is causing the most resistance in your body. The most unease, the most dis-ease.

Once you are no longer focused in a fearful, angry way on wrongs, you can focus in a joyful, happy way on rights. And pretty soon your cup will runneth over with love…

GENEROSITY

The 'abundance versus poverty' game is the most significant challenge on this planet. Abundance is usually assumed to mean money, but everything flows in abundance, or it doesn't flow, which is lack. Time, food, happiness, relationships, creativity and in fact everything is an energy which we allow to flow, or we don't. Abundance is the complete expression of Source energy, and lack is the blocking of Source energy. The easiest way to unblock abundance is to be generous.

Generosity connects us to our true essence of Divine and makes us feel good. But, only if we can be generous without guilt or regret. Pure generosity is balanced, in that it doesn't take from you to give to another. It is an overflowing of love; it is an act of opening your heart.

Practice generosity knowing that when you give, you shall receive. The flow of Source energy is like water and fills immediately any space that appears. Start by giving to yourself. Then, practice giving to family and friends, and then practice giving to strangers. Recognize and enjoy the pleasure you receive from giving. Empower yourself with love and the expression of love; generosity. What a contribution to humanity you will be.

But do not give when you think you 'should,' and do not give when you are feeling 'lack' within yourself. Find the balance of that, and work out when you have a surplus to give and give unconditionally then. Give when you are feeling abundant and clear, and you will receive more abundance and clarity.

Do not fear giving to others, decide to be generous and activate the flow of abundance, which will serve you and all around you. Giving, and sharing love, abundantly feeds our soul and humanity as a whole. Remember you receive what you transmit, so when you are giving to others, you are also giving to yourself. Feel the emotion of abundance, feel the give and take.

Receive open-heartedly, only then can you give open-heartedly. You can't give away something that you don't have to give. If you have fear, then that is what you will give away, in the form of anger, resentment, abandonment, worry, etc. If you are with someone who can't give you love, then they don't have it to give away. You can love yourself, so you have love, and then you can give it away to them. Then they will have love, and then they can choose to give some back to you.

Be generous with love to yourself and others. Be generous with your time to yourself and others. Be generous with your abundance to yourself and others. The more you give, the more you receive. So, you had better practice receiving. If you have come from a belief that states you are not worthy, you are going to want to practice being worthy and receiving. At every opportunity receive another's generosity with gratitude. Acknowledge how good it feels to give, and allow another to experience that.

Declare to the Universe, "I am worthy." "I am receiving with an open-heart and open arms." "I am generous." "I am kind."

Become a beacon of light, with your crown shining bright and your feet deeply rooted. Be a beacon for yourself first, and others second. This is not selfish; this is self-full. If we all practiced being self-full on our planet, there would be no need to feel a lack.

Do not think or say negative think things about yourself. Do not tell yourself you are not good enough. Focus instead on what is positive and loving. Every negative word you think and speak adds to the toxins within you, and every positive word dissolves the poison and switches on tonics. Compliment yourself every time you look in the mirror.

Use compliments like a magic wand. Share the love! Bless others around you with a divine transmission of love from your heart. Find something to compliment people on. Praise them and make them feel appreciated. Smile at them widely; give an energetic gift from your heart to theirs. They may never be able to return the compliment, but that is because their cup is empty. Be generous and overflow your cup with no expectation of reciprocation.

Be attentive when someone is talking to you; listen carefully without interrupting. Celebrate another's success, be joyful and don't compare their achievements with yours. Show sympathy when someone needs it, and only offer advice when specifically asked. Be respectful and loving, allow others to find their own path. Practice patience and tolerance, and hold no expectations or judgments. Be generous with your smile, put your glow on and beam generously to all around you.

THIRD ADVENTURE

So, here you are at the third and final adventure. You have climbed mountains and waded through rivers. You have danced in the light, and in the shadows. You have sunk your roots into the depths of Mother Earth and crowned yourself with Source. You love yourself and are happy to own it. You are vibrating higher now than when you first started out on the Love Revolution.

By now you have mastered the Switch Breath and therefore your knee-jerk reactions to life. You have learned how to sit without expectation and judgment, and allowed the process of unraveling to occur. You have been teaching your body, mind, and heart to relax, and you are getting used to feeling happy. You are feeling the love!

You are naturally moving more regularly into coherence, a powerful state when your heart and your brain are aligned, and all your systems are positively maximized. Coherence allows us to experience higher emotional states in our meditation like rapture and bliss, and in our everyday lives as gratitude, satisfaction, and happiness.

Your new set point of coherence is also fabulous for your beautiful body as it boosts your immunity system, charges your cells, and your happiness makes you glow. You can now tell your friends you are *youthing* not aging. Now doesn't that give you a boost of warm fuzzies!

When you are coherent, you are powerful. By holding a high vibration, you are also attracting others to entrain to your frequency. You are positively affecting your relationships by simply holding love energetically. Remember the power the heart has to connect to and change the atoms around it.

It's time to take responsibility for the energy you carry with you. Own your power! Remember we are all energy and we are all connected in this Universe. Watch your words and your moods. Continue to state, "I love myself!"

Don't stop now… it's just getting really interesting. If you haven't already, you are very soon going to see the results of your new beliefs. Once you are vibrating on the "I love myself!" vibration, you begin transmitting the essence of who you truly are, which opens you up to the realm of infinite possibilities.

This next practice has you sitting in the heart space, connecting the breath above and below, and then moving into heart expression. You are going to experience open-heartedness and all the bliss that brings. You are going to allow your true self to transmit your heart's desire, and receive Universal love, which you may never have experienced before. You are going to experience Oneness.

The more you tune yourself into your heart space, the higher the vibration rate within your body. You will become light. Every single one of your trillions of cells can store and utilize light, and when your cells are lit up, so too is your DNA. By lighting up your cells, you resonate with divine Source and fill yourself up with pure potentiality.

So let's get started…

PRACTICE

Find your seat and do the Switch Breath. Then slowly and surely move through the meditation, settling into your body space and your head space. Feel yourself rooted in Mother Earth and crowned by Spirit. Feel the breath inhaling from both ends of your body and into your heart space. And then feel the breath exhaling and exiting out of your crown and your roots.

When you are ready, it is time to move on. Bring your awareness and your connection to your heart space. Bring your hand to your heart space and feel the movement of the breath here. The expansion, and the contraction of the breath in the heart space.

Focus on the depth of the enjoyment of the breathing. Feel alive and breathe. Feel the joy of being here *now*. Tune into that and turn it up. Feel how that vibration feels. It is a merging of Mother Earth with divine Source. Tune in and turn it up again. You are now connected above and below, full of Source energy and rooted firmly in Mother Earth. Tune in and turn it up again. Feel the love, feel gratitude for the love. Tune in and turn it up again. There is enough love in you to heal the whole planet.

Feel the warmth growing in your heart space and overflowing into your body.

It is now time to open your heart. Remove your hand and return it to your lap. Feel the heart space open and expand. Start softly and surely moving the energy in and out of the heart with your breath. Inhale into the heart and exhale out of the heart.

Feel the Oneness with the Universe. Feel the Oneness with all of humanity.

Sit here as long as you want, and when you start becoming aware again of your individuality, begin to bring the breath back into the belly slowly. Place your hand here if you want some help grounding. Do not come back quickly; take as long as you can. There has been a huge energetic transference, and there is a settling taking place.

Sit with eyes shut, breathing softly into the belly until the cells settle down.

Start to listen to noises outside of your body, and start tuning yourself to your surroundings. Wiggle your toes and your fingers. Softly roll your head. When it feels like it is time, open your eyes and softly look at the space you sit in, noticing how everything seems different, as your perspective has shifted.

When you are ready, get up and stretch, and go and drink a big glass of water. Water is what cells need to transmute, to shift from one state to another. I also recommend you go and look in the mirror, "Hello lovely!!!"

5

SURRENDER YOURSELF IN LOVE

CONGRATULATIONS

YOU HAVE REACHED THE end of the Love Revolution; I want you to pat yourself on the back. You will have taken two steps forward, and one step back, (or one step forward and two steps back), as you journeyed through this process. I call this the Cha Cha Cha of life, and I invite you to continue to enjoy the dance.

The Love Revolution is more than a book; it is a movement that will continue for you, as you continue through life. You may even want to turn back to the beginning and start the book again; now you have a clearer perception of who you *truly* are. You have learned a lot about yourself, and you have learned how to love and accept yourself. You are practicing how to love yourself, no matter what. That is true enlightenment.

The Love Revolution is an adventure that will continue to unfold through your life, a life you cannot even begin to imagine. You *now* have the ability to tune yourself up from fear to love. And when you are free of your fears, you are also free of any situations that engage those fears. Life has become simpler, with less drama and stress. Now all you have to do is surrender.

Ahhhhhhhhh…

Can you feel the relief of that?

I see you in a boat, on the ocean of divine Source energy. To surrender is to lie down in your boat, and to allow the Universe to propel you. Surrender your will to divine will. Your destination is on the horizon, and all the little details of getting there are none of your concern. Know you are safe, and all is well.

The Universe has your journey covered, and as long as you relax in your boat and surrender to the flow of Source, all will be well. Do not allow yourself to get wrecked on the shores of 'doubt' by trying to manage your boat yourself. Have faith that the Universe knows where you want to go, and knows how to get you there. You are sailing into a beautiful future.

Your thoughts are energy, and like attracts like. Whatever you are paying attention to is where you are connecting. When you are meditating, you are connecting with others who are meditating. When you are loving, you are connecting with others who are loving. Hanging out in the frequency of love is the best, and the only way to heal the planet. The only way to impact what is going on 'out there' is by deciding to control what is happening 'in here.'

So, be ever more conscious in your life. Be present to yourself and to the frequency you are transmitting. Remain responsible always for how you are thinking and acting, responsible for what you are putting your attention on. Remember your focus is your superpower. Always ask yourself, "What am I paying attention to...?" If it is less than love, use the Switch breath. Play the old switcheroo. Let life get better and better. Allow yourself to receive the goodness. You deserve it, and so much more.

Every morning, before you arise, ask yourself, "What sort of day do I want?" Set your frequency, and then get up and gratefully live your lovely life. Always make time for your meditation practice and your journal of gratitude. Continue to say "I love myself!" internally and out loud, especially if you have had a bad day.

Knock yourself out (figuratively speaking!) and start an exercise program too. I recommend Yoga as it aligns your body with your mind and soul, and stretches you out of contraction into expansion. But whatever turns you on is perfect. Walk your talk on the Love Revolution. *Be* healthy, happy and whole.

Dream and scheme **big** plans. Dream with no limitations, knowing anything and everything is possible. Do not be tempted to share your dreams with anyone, not unless they, like you, are truly understanding of the power of love, as they may think you are a little mad and lovingly (in their eyes) deflate you. Keep your dreams close to your heart, as they are your heart's desires.

When you feel doubt, take time to go through the meditation to tune yourself up, and then surrender. Miracles happen when you surrender.

The Universe is perfectly weaving the perfect reality to fulfill your perfect desires perfectly, bigger and better than you could ever organize. Lighten up and have fun on this adventure that is your life. Surrender all the boring details to the Universe. Trust the flow of Source and relax! There is a wind in your sails. The momentum of the work you have already done will continue to pull you, like a tide, towards an ever brighter, ever lighter you. So *always* look forward to abundance, *never* look back at lack.

Own your life and your blessings by allowing things to come to you - don't worry about how and when. Give up waiting, and move forward happily. Get out of the way of yourself. Waiting is a huge block, a frequency of resistance between you and your dream manifestations. It keeps what you desire on hold. So give up waiting, and instead, celebrate your Cha Cha Cha through life, and look forward to the "Ta Daaa!" moments.

And now to the final frontier...

PRACTICE

Do the Switch Breath and slowly and surely move through the meditation, settling into your body space, head space, and heart space. Feel yourself rooted in Mother Earth, crowned by Spirit and expressing from the heart.

As you practice, you will get quicker as you move through the body, head and heart spaces. But don't rush!

If you speed through you will not be able to truly and deeply surrender.

When you have tuned yourself as high as you can today, all I ask you to do is let go. Let go of all control and instruction, and rest and relax in the grace of the space, the essence of who you truly are. Your *true* self.

Just get in your boat and lie down. Surrender and allow the flow of Source to float you towards the light. Surrender your will to divine will.

Be here now, breathing and flowing. Feel the love.

Feel the connection to the Universal field that surrounds you, and breathe Source energy in from the field, and out into the field. Boundaries are softening, and the sense of Oneness with the Universe is increasing. You are coherent *within* the body, and you are coherent *without* the body.

Allow thoughts to arrive and receive the inspiration. Ask, "What is it you want to tell me?" and "What do I need to know?" Also, "Where do you want me to go today?" and "What do you want me to do?"

Sit for as long as you feel surrendered. Some days will be longer than others. Set an alarm if time is going to be a worry for you.

Come back slowly. Do not bounce back into life, or life may bounce you back.

Start by feeling the chair underneath you, and the floor under your feet. Listen to the noises around you and tune yourself back into your surroundings.

Wiggle, stretch and move with your eyes still shut. Open the eyes once you are completely back in the body. Slowly look around at the space that you sit in, and then at you in the space. Take some big belly breaths and then get up and get on with your day, knowing you that are grounded, crowned, open-hearted and surrendered to Source energy. All is well!

FINAL NOTE

Thank you for being a part of the Love Revolution, and thank you for oozing love along your way. Thank you for joining other Love Revolutionaries on the mission to clean up our vibration and meditate in love, therefore healing the world around us, and beyond. Thank you for being on the leading edge of consciousness and being the change you want to see. Thank you for being love.

Here are some last words of wisdom...

Fill your boots, stand tall, and don't forget your crown!
Express from your brave and powerful heart.
Smile and always remember…

The world is your oyster, and you are the pearl.

Arohanui - much love - Erin

Visit the website
theloverevolution.online
to hear the audible version of the meditation.

ilovemyself
are the magic words.

COMPLETE PRACTISE

Switch Breath~

Eyes open and softly focused.

Inhale through the nose for a count of 4.

Hold for a count of 4.

Exhale through the mouth for a count of 4.

Hold for a count of 4.

Repeat for 4 breaths.

Feel the Switch shift inside.

Body Space~

Sit, with your eyes softly gazing.

Find comfort, move towards deeper comfort.

Acknowledge that you are transitioning into meditation.

Feel the relaxation arriving.

When it feels right, softly close your eyes.

Feel the weight of your body on the seat.

Relax deeper into your body.

Watch the breath in the belly.

Root yourself in Mother Earth.

Count 1 to 10, again and again.

Feel the support of Mother Earth.

Head Space~

Move awareness to the head space.

Watch the breath in the head.

Allow Source energy to flow in the top of the head.

Feel and see this energy as light.

Receive this light into every cell of your body.

Light up your cells.

Crown yourself with light.

Enjoy the inspiration.

Heart Space~

Move your awareness to the heart space.

Watch the breath in the heart.

Feel the joy of being in your heart.

Tune in and turn it up.

Feel the love, and feel gratitude for the love.

Tune in and turn it up.

Open your heart.

Breathe through your heart.

Feel the Oneness.

Surrender~

Let all control go and relax deeper.

Surrender your will to divine will.

You are grounded, crowned and openhearted.

Just sit. Just BE.

Printed in the United States
By Bookmasters